'LOOKING WITHIN'

India has produced some of the world's greatest religious leaders, sages, saints, philosophers and spiritual thinkers. They were monks, nuns and renunciates, nationalists and reformers. No one religion had a monopoly on them. They range from Mahavira and Buddha, who lived over 2,500 years ago, to medieval saints like Chishti, Avvaiyar and Guru Nanak, to more recent philosophers and religious icons such as Vivekananda, Ramakrishna, Saint Teresa and many others. The spiritual and philosophical heritage they left behind is India's gift to all Indians and the world.

In the 'Life Lessons' series we publish the essential teachings of some of India's best-known spiritual teachers, along with commentaries and biographical notes. Each book will be a handy companion to help the reader along the difficult pathways of life.

Also in Aleph 'Life Lessons'

'You Are the Supreme Light': Life Lessons from Adi Shankara

'Be Present in Every Moment': Life Lessons from Moinuddin Chishti

'The Light in All is One': Life Lessons from Guru Nanak

'Live and Let Others Live': Life Lessons from Mahavira

'LOOKING WITHIN'

~

LIFE LESSONS FROM

LAL DED

EDITED BY

Shonaleeka Kaul

ALEPH

ALEPH BOOK COMPANY
An independent publishing firm
promoted by ***Rupa Publications India***

First published in India in 2019
by Aleph Book Company
7/16 Ansari Road, Daryaganj
New Delhi 110 002

ISBN: 978-93-88292-70-2

1 3 5 7 9 10 8 6 4 2

Printed at Parksons Graphics Pvt. Ltd, Mumbai

Śrīkṛṣṇārpaṇamastu

In memory of

Babu Bhai and Buddoo

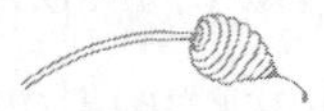

SERIES INTRODUCTION

India has produced some of the world's greatest religious leaders, sages, saints, philosophers and spiritual thinkers. They were monks, nuns and renunciates, nationalists and reformers. No one religion had a monopoly on them. They range from Mahavira and Buddha, who lived over 2,500 years ago, to medieval saints like Chishti, Avvaiyar and Guru Nanak, to more recent philosophers and religious icons such as Vivekananda, Ramakrishna, Saint Teresa and many others. Each of them touched the lives of the people they lived among and the generations that followed. They inspired devotees and followers with their erudition and wisdom. The spiritual and philosophical heritage they left behind is India's gift to all Indians and the world.

Through the 'Life Lessons' series we will examine the teachings of some of India's best-known spiritual teachers. Each book will be a handy companion to help the reader along the difficult pathways of life.

Happiness and sorrow are unavoidable. The world is a place of trials and problems recur in every generation. Is suffering a necessary part of human life? How can one overcome suffering? Can hardship make a person stronger? What is happiness? Everybody wants to be happy, but how does one achieve this state? Does happiness come from vast riches and great achievements or does it come from the satisfaction of the soul? Is worldly success more important or is it fulfilment that one should seek?

These and similar questions vex every individual and have preoccupied the minds of philosophers and religious savants down the ages. The answers that these great souls found to life's conundrums occupy entire libraries worth of books and texts. This series is culled from their essential teachings and will present to readers some of the greatest truths to be found in India's spiritual heritage in a simple and accessible way. It is to be hoped that what you find here will prompt you to go deeper into the life and work of those who plumbed life's greatest mysteries.

Walking in the footsteps of these great men and women can take each of us to greater heights of knowledge, wisdom and understanding. They can teach us how to find happiness and peace and the true meaning of well-being and success. Most of all, they can teach us how to value one another and cherish the holy gift of life.

INTRODUCTION

Who was Lal Ded?* Fittingly for someone who espoused the insignificance of worldly identities, little is known about this Shaiva mystic saint except that she lived in Kashmir, probably in the fourteenth century. Her relative anonymity notwithstanding, perhaps there isn't a single Kashmiri who has not heard of Lal Ded (Granny Lal) or Lal Maej (Mother Lal), whose full name was Lalleshwari, or of her

*Lal is pronounced with a short a and a double l, like in gull. Ded in Kashmiri is an affectionate reference for an older woman.

many sayings that have seeped far and wide into popular usage. Such was the love and respect in which she was held by the masses in Kashmir that much later texts in Persian, like the *Tazkirat ul Arifin* and the *Tarikh I Azami*, written by Muslim scholars between the sixteenth and eighteenth centuries, were also impelled to mention her. In fact, her near-contemporary, the Islamic Sufi saint Sheikh Nooruddin or Nund Rishi, as he came to be known, was deeply influenced by Lal's teachings and the order he founded came to be known as the Rishi-Sufi order, representing the syncretism for which Kashmir was once famous. It is worth noting, however, that Lal Ded herself did not found any movement or order of followers; she came and went alone, a wanderer—her message meant for the redemption of the individual soul.

The texts mentioned above provide us with some legendary biographical details about Lal, such as her birth in a Brahmin family of Pandrethan (near Srinagar), an early, bad marriage and many domestic hardships faced in her marital home, prompting a turn to spirituality. She is said to have been guided in this by a guru, Siddha Srikantha or Siddhamol (Enlightened Father). However, there is no way to know if all (or any) of this is true, for Lal's own verses in the Kashmiri tongue, known as vaakhs (literally 'sayings' or 'utterances', from the Sanskrit vaak), do not provide any such information. They do, however, refer to her guru. In any case, as scholars have pointed out, the greatness of Lal is hardly limited to her life story, as we shall see.

Though not speaking specifically about her own life, Lal's vaakhs are deeply personal. In these vaakhs, she uses the first person and also names herself frequently, using her shorter, pet name. For example, the phrase 'I, Lal' or even 'Lalli' is a common refrain in the vaakhs, prefacing her sayings in a conversational style—where the conversation is often with herself. Seen in other mystics as well, talking to herself in her vaakhs is a technique that points to Lal Ded's central teaching of turning inwards to arrive at life's greatest truths. Thus she says:

My guru said just one thing:
'Turn within, turn within!'

This was Lal's sole education:
To learn to leap inside herself.

I rejected every false belief,
immersed myself in my inner voice alone.
Ultimately I saw myself looking
deeply into my Self.
And knew it to be You, God, in every speck.

Indeed, Lal's vaakhs take you on an individual's journey through the woes of the human condition, disillusionment with the world, an anguished search for God, and, ultimately, to the realization of the highest truth that liberates. They move from the outer to the inner world and take the listener/reader on this voyage too. The vaakhs translated in this book (each vaakh is a four-line lyrical verse, rendered in a colloquial style)* are also arranged into four sections accordingly: The first, Life of Illusions, describes how we are mired in emotional and social attachments and material pursuits, and the futility of these attachments. The second section, The Search, describes the process of an individual wearying of the material life and seeking a way out by exploring different conventional paths, to no avail. The third, The Realization, describes Lal's breakthrough moment when she experienced pure consciousness and bliss. And, finally, section four, The Way, brings together Lal's advice on how to go about realizing one's true Self and gaining liberation.

---

*At places in this book the vaakhs in translation have spilled into five, six or seven lines, due to constraints of page size.

Again, despite being such a personal narration, Lal's life lessons are universal. Her observations on the transience and futility of material pursuits and the emotions they generate, like greed, anger, pride and fear, apply to all of us. All of us have also known the sufferings involved in the wake of even positive emotions, such as worldly love and attachments. The terror and certainty of death haunt all humans, even the powerful and the rich, as Lal reminds us. Her frantic search for God and repeated failures while trying out the myriad paths to Him ring true to the experience of those of us who are spiritually inclined.

Therefore, despite the profundity of her teachings, her humanism makes it easy to relate to Lal. This explains why her sayings have been preserved, for the most part, not in any textual tradition but through popular collective memory, in songs, proverbs and hymns repeated by all strata of Kashmiris, generation after generation, over the six centuries since she walked the earth. In fact, these vaakhs that were strewn through popular culture were collected and compiled by various Kashmiri Pandit and British scholars only as recently as the nineteenth century. In this regard it is interesting to note that Lal's vaakhs constitute one of the earliest compositions in the history of the Kashmiri tongue, after the thirteenth-century *Mahanaya Prakash*, thereby playing a pioneering role in the emergence and shaping of Kashmiri language and literature.

Despite her tremendous appeal among

common people, Lal was quite uncommon, the most exceptional aspect of her life being her spectacular realization of God—or rather of pure consciousness that transcends even the gods. She describes the splendour and ecstasy of that realization in her own words and readers will get a taste of it in the third section of her verses in this book. For example, she says:

Like gold when burnished loses all impurities.
I glowed bright in the fire of
pure consciousness.
Melting in love,
I found the fog of delusion lift
as the sun rose right beside me!

Pure consciousness was such bliss,
all veils of illusion and thought lifted.
Spontaneously I realized my whole Self.
And Lal bloomed like a lotus in the mud.

What was Lal really trying to convey and why? What was her philosophy and what her prescription? As her vaakhs suggest, Lal belongs to the Trika school of Kashmiri Shaiva mysticism or devotional Shivadvaita, which originated no later than the eighth century CE. Shiva-shakti worship in Kashmir dates to at least the second century CE, as glimpsed in gold coins of the period that depict Shiva, trident in hand and tiger sprawled at his feet. Colossal Shiva lingas as well as sculptures of Maheshvara as Bhuteshvara, and of members of Shiva's divine family, such as Durga, Ganesha and Kartikeya, are also to be found in the valley from at least the fifth century CE. In fact, the *Nilamata Purana*, composed in Sanskrit in the eighth century CE and the earliest extant account of Kashmir's origins and sacred geography, tells us that Kashmir was founded from a primordial lake (Satisaras) where Sati, the consort of Shiva, resided. The *Nilamata* as well as Kalhana's *Rajatarangini* (twelfth century CE), the earliest surviving history of Kashmir, unambiguously state that the valley of Kashmir is Parvati herself and the king of Kashmir but a portion of Shiva.

Alongside this theistic and iconographic form of Shaivism, there developed a deeply monist strand of philosophy in Kashmir that identified Shiva as pure consciousness. This school, that came to be called Pratyabhijna (Recognition) or Trika (triad of Shiva, Shakti and Nara), was represented in the works of great scholar-siddhas like Bhatta Narayana (eighth century), Utpaladeva (ninth century), Abhinavagupta (tenth to eleventh centuries) and Shitikantha (thirteenth century). Lal Ded belongs to this line of realized souls as do the other great Kashmiri mystics, like Roopa Bhavani (seventeenth century) and Lakshman Joo (twentieth century), who expounded the same continuous tradition long after Lal.

What is Trika? Though it is difficult to render this highly sophisticated belief system in simple terms, we can explain it thus: all of creation is replete with one indivisible super consciousness called Parama Shiva (the supreme principle). But human beings do not realize this truth since their intellect is clouded by delusions or amnesia induced by a sensory or material life. This makes them mistakenly identify themselves with their worldly forms and roles, causing them a great deal of suffering in the process, and obscuring their real identity, which is one with God, who is formless, nameless, pure consciousness.

In Lal's vaakhs, she urges a simple (saral) and spontaneous (sahaj) realization or recognition of this ultimate reality by turning inwards. This is because, according to her, Shiva himself is subtle and spontaneous and resides within each of us. Thus people could not and should not be discriminated against on the basis of their outward faith or customs. As Lal puts it:

Shiva is the sole reality and witness
in whichever direction you look.
Don't distinguish the Brahmin and
the Muslim then.
If you're a Trika, go within,
know only yourself!

The inclusivism of Lal's monism and of Kashmiri Shaivism is thus great indeed.

Lal also rejects the role of outward rituals and ostentation (including animal sacrifice) or pilgrimage and also extreme asceticism (including fasting and other forms of mortification of the human body) to attain this truth. She says:

To fly through the air
or stop the flow of gushing waters,

to douse fire by incantation
or produce milk from a wooden cow—
all such miracles
and show of spiritual prowess
are but chicanery and deceit!

What is the point of forsaking the home
and heading to the forest?
Why smear sacred ash
and ointments on yourself?
You are fine just the way you are!
Bear God in your heart, that's all it takes!

Indeed, Lal Ded's way is the pathless path (nishpath). All that it requires is an intense, all-consuming love for God even as we go about our daily lives—a longing for Him who, according to Lal, Himself seeks out the seeker.

Why fear, oh Self,
when the Eternal itself seeks you out?
Know not whom or ask why,
just heed the call when it comes.

God's grace and an intent concentration on the Self through observing the inflow and outflow of one's breath, which she describes as the natural mantra (ajapa gayatri), leads to the direct experience (anubhav) of the ultimate consciousness. Thus, according to Lal, liberation is Self-realization—an expansion of the indivisible Self to include the whole universe by seeing beyond all dualities and differences in it. Further, she tells us that pure consciousness is a state of nothingness (shunya ati shunya), a state of sheer bliss and radiance. Lal explains:

I enquired from my guru a thousand times:
What, after all, does nothingness mean?
He was quiet; I gave up and quietened too.
And it is from that silence, at last,
that no-thing emerged!

Practices (tantra) gave way to
knowledge (mantra).
Knowledge dissolved into consciousness.
When consciousness dissolved,
nothing remained.
Nothingness dissolved into nothingness!

One who experiences this state of nothingness

or pure consciousness no longer knows any fear or grief, not even of death, and hence becomes genuinely free (swatantra) within one's lifetime. Such a realized soul is known as jivan mukta. Lal, having tasted the nectar of the eternal truth, and suffused with Shiva (shiva-vyapti), was truly liberated. In her own words:

Alert, when Lal entered her heart
she witnessed the union of
Shiva and Shakti there!
She dissolved into an ocean of nectar.
Transcending life while still alive thus,
Death had no business with Lal anymore!

The life lessons that one can learn from Lal Ded are not only spiritual; they are also deeply ethical and inspiring. Here was a brave, young, solitary woman, with a profound understanding of the human condition, striving with acuity and determination to find a way out of the confusing morass of everyday life, social relations, and emotional entanglements to the clarity and bliss of self-discovery. As her verses indicate, she stood aloof and alone in the face of apparent social censure for being such an intrepid and unconventional woman—and became her own light! Thus she says:

Whether the world venerates me or shuns me
I alone will bear the consequences
of my detached actions,
which are offered to my own Self.
So wherever I go, I will prosper!

Let people abuse and taunt me.
Or let them shower petals in adoration.
Nothing affects me.
I am pure consciousness.

Only when I can withstand censure
will my inhibitions break down.
Let my pride be torn asunder!
Let not attacks bother me!

No ordinary person is capable of such exceptional self-awareness and fortitude. This is why Lal's greatness and qualities such as indomitable courage, steely perseverance, and scintillating intellect can hardly be explained by any domestic challenges she may have faced in her early life. Lal was perhaps, above all, an extraordinary individual who rose high above the petty concerns and bondage of society in her pursuit of Self-realization. As she says: 'When the inner light lit up within me, off went the light outside.'

What is even more fascinating is that the dazzling knowledge she arrived at was not through being highly educated or versed in scriptures or complex ritual techniques (mantra, tantra). As she avers, 'I was born simple and simple I will die.' Hence, in a strong reminder of that other great Indian saint from the fifteenth century, Kabir, who, though unlettered, preached high Upanishadic Advaita* in the simplest of tongues on the streets of Banaras, Lal's knowledge of the true nature of reality

*Advaita or non-dualism is the idea that the soul (atman) and the highest metaphysical reality (brahman) are one.

and the Self was intuitive and experiential. She belongs to a long line of brilliant and pious souls that came from the sacred land of Kashmir.

In our consumerist and hyper-connected modern world today, we are ironically cut off from our own inner selves. As a result, we suffer as a society from great violence and turmoil. Today, more than ever before therefore, Lal Ded's luminous utterances shine brightly from across the centuries as a beacon of salvation and show us the way to redeem our true selves.

I

LIFE OF ILLUSIONS

I know not from where I have come and how.
Nor where and how I will go hereafter.
What wealth will serve me on this journey?
How does one trust this precarious breath?

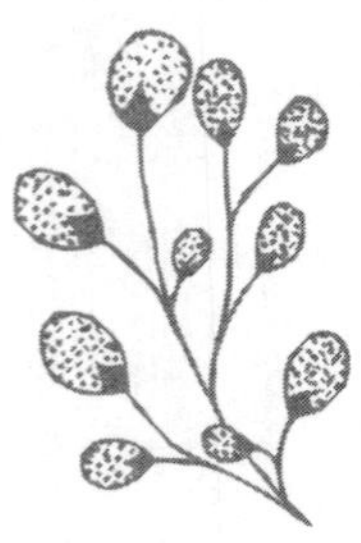

Oh why did I lose myself
in attachment to others!
Why did I see falsehood as truth?
Deluded, in thrall to the senses now,
one is stuck in the cycle of birth and death.

Why did I let myself sink in a
sea of attachments?
Slush and mire now abound.
The shore is long lost sight of.
In the end we will all die.
Who will release us from the fear of death?

The foundation of your life is but quicksand,
your attachments illusory.
Hoard all that you wish,
you will have to leave it all behind.
Why then are you immersed in these things?

Why do you mould oars out of sand?
Can you row your boat with these?
Can your fate, death, be averted in any way
when it has been decreed for sure by God?

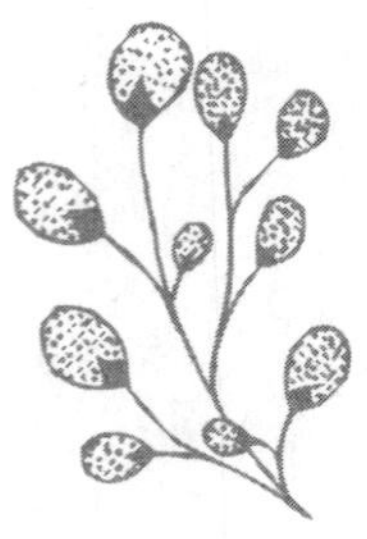

I saw a learned man dying
of want and starvation.
And, on the other hand,
an affluent fool beating up his chef.
Seeing these paradoxes of life,
disillusionment with the world
is inevitable for Lal.

You are so lost in greed and attachment to
things, I weep for you.
Your armour-clad ship of life
will be gone in a moment.
Why don't you recognize your true Self?

Chariots, thrones, pomp and pleasure
are forever, you think.
Why then is the fear of death
never far from you?

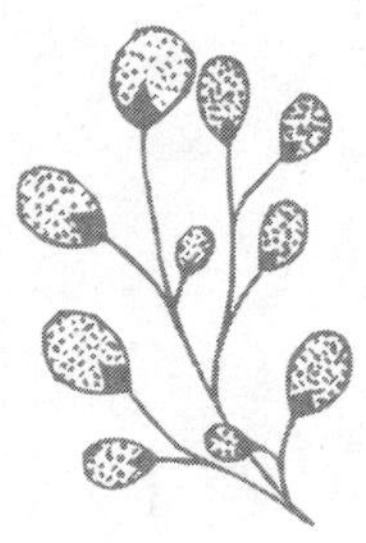

Like a bow made of wood that won't bend
and arrows of hollow reed,
like a badly built house,
or a shop without a vendor,
life without consciousness is futile.

Drunk on the ocean of worldly pursuits
many are the games I have played,
forms I have taken,
many the births and deaths endured.
Why? What is wrong with me?
When I am Shakti herself!

Like water washes away unbaked clay
worldly temptations assail me.
With a delicate thread I tow my boat,
may God help ferry me!

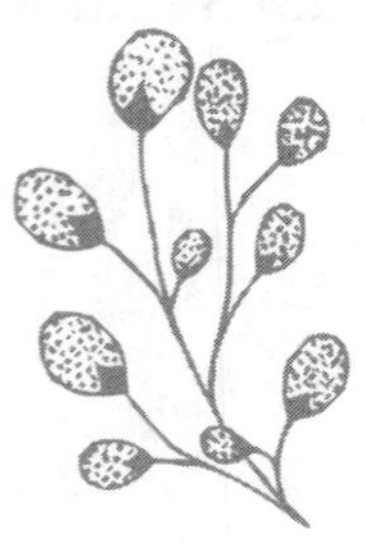

II

THE SEARCH

I arrived a traveller. The day is now ended.
God is not by my side,
how will I find my way home?
All around me are meaningless things.
With whose help can I possibly cross over?

I have not known wealth since birth
nor luxuries and greed for them.
Content with little food, poverty and hardship,
all I have known is love for God.

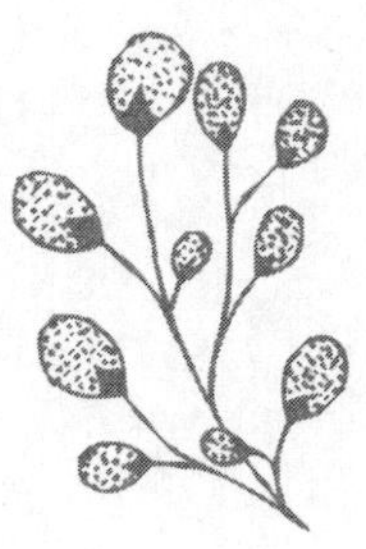

I was born simple and simple I will die.
The crooked world is of no interest to me.
Tuned to God constantly
since the beginning of time,
aware and in love, no anxiety plagues me.

I recited mantras till my palate wore thin.
I turned the prayer bead
till my fingers bruised.
Yet I could do no justice to you, God!
For the realization of oneness with You and
others eluded me.

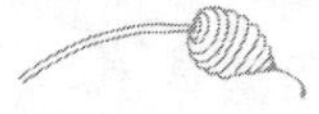

All I did was think about the body,
never once about what lies beyond.
I am no different from You—
never did this dawn on me!

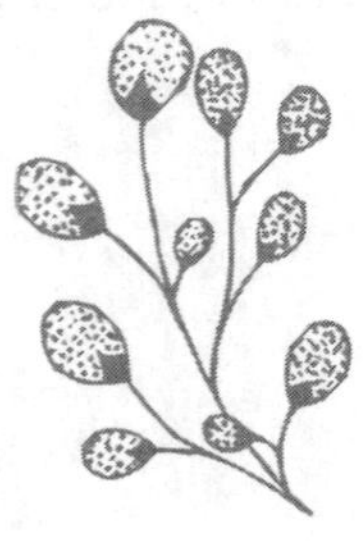

Shed deceit, caprice, and untruth,
I tell myself.
Know that Shiva alone resides in one and all.
Why distinguish people then
by their food, drink and customs?

I called out for Him hundreds of times
Sought Him so hard, I became distraught.
Not a door opened anywhere I turned.
Yet I sat waiting, keeping vigil.

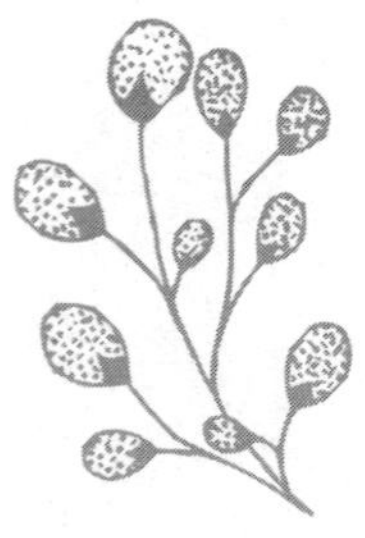

Why fear, oh Self,
when the Eternal itself seeks you out?
Know not whom or ask why,
just heed the call when it comes.

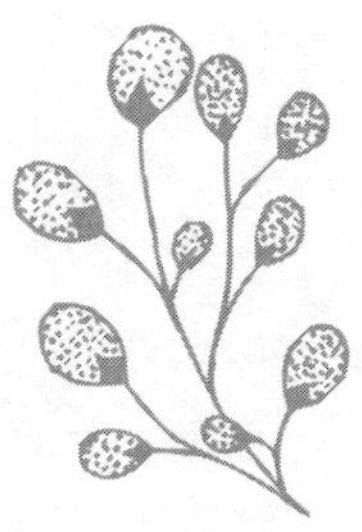

I enquired from my guru a thousand times:
What, after all, does nothingness mean?
He was quiet; I gave up and quietened too.
And it was from that silence, at last,
that no-thing emerged!

When other cravings ceased,
peace came to me.
I prepared my heart in the pestle of love.
Then emblazoned it and partook of it.
Now if I live or die, it's all the same to me!

Treading hundreds of paths to find God
the flesh of my feet wore out—in vain.
Then the One alone showed me
the Only Way.
Oh how my story will tantalize
all who hear it!

My guru said just one thing:
'Turn within, turn within!'
This was Lal's sole education:
To learn to leap inside herself.

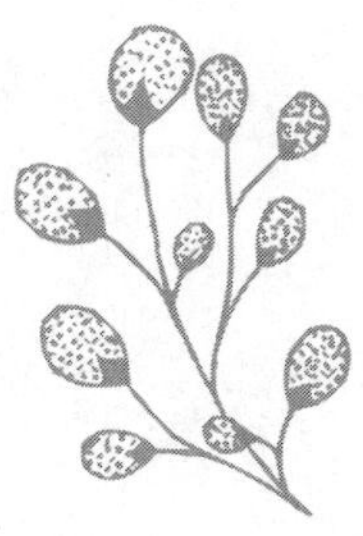

I rejected every false belief,
immersed myself in my inner voice alone.
Ultimately I saw myself
looking deeply into my Self.
And knew it to be You, God, in every speck.

Rising at dawn, awash with the pain of love,
I exhorted my heart to call out to Him!
Lal, Lal, Lal! cried I, and He awoke!
United with Him now I am pure and blessed.

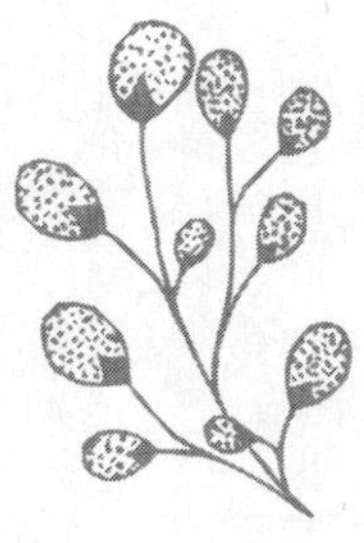

Lost in His love, I, Lal,
looked everywhere for Him.
But then found Him right here, at home
the day I learnt to tell transience
from permanence.

When the inner light lit up within me,
off went the light outside.
In the darkness
I seized Him and held Him tight!

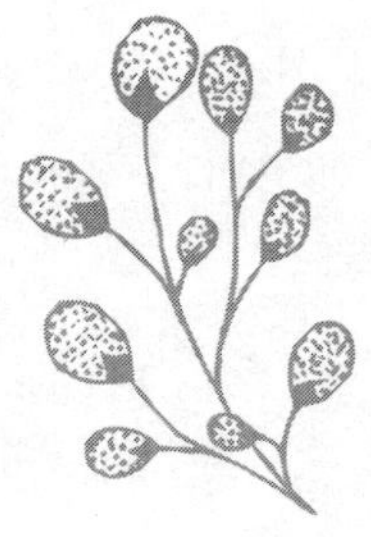

I searched in vain for my inner Self
in all schools of esoteric knowledge.
On actually drowning in the experience of Self
I found it's there for the taking—
if only people cared!

When the mirror of my heart was cleansed
I gained my true identity.
I found Him near each and everyone
and knew He is all there is!

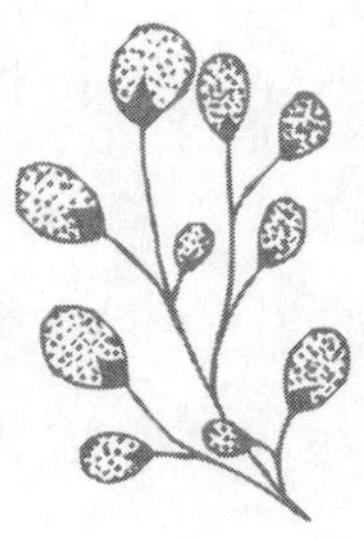

Let people abuse and taunt me.
Or let them shower petals in adoration.
Nothing affects me.
I am pure consciousness.

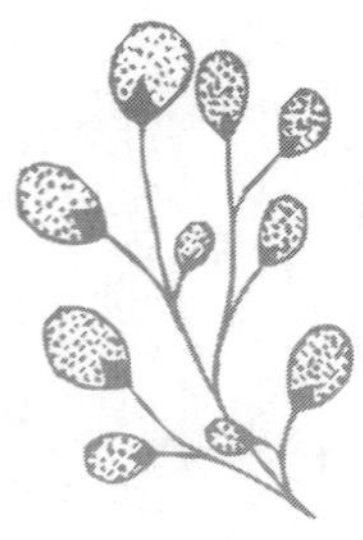

Only when I can withstand censure
will my inhibitions break down.
Let my pride be torn asunder!
Let not attacks bother me!

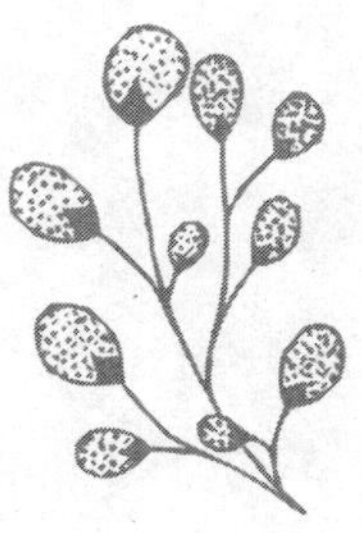

To one who dwells inside herself
unbearable taunts cause no grief.
If I am a devotee of Shiva
no dirt can cling to my mirror.

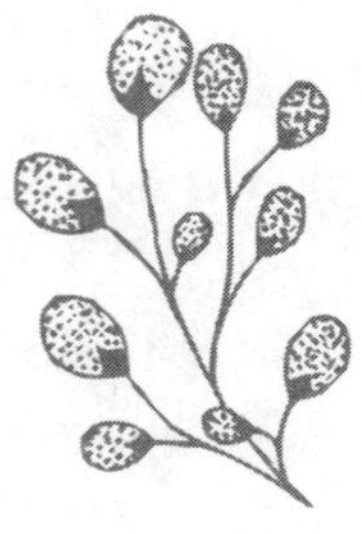

Whether the world venerates me or shuns me
I alone will bear the consequences
of my detached actions,
which are offered to my own Self.
So wherever I go, I will prosper!

Steeped in Shiva
Lal's body and mind emerged like new.
The consciousness and the objective world
all steeped in Shiva, appeared new.

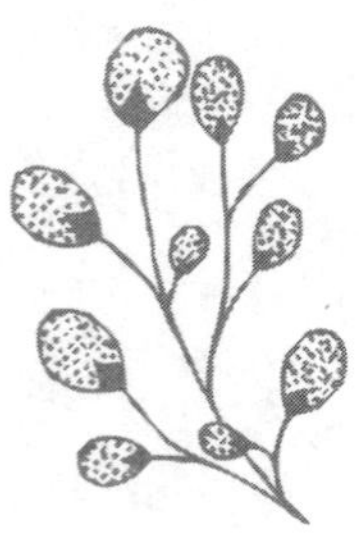

Whatever acts I performed
became offerings to God.
Whatever utterances I spoke became prayer.
Whatever the body consumed
became oblations.
This is the way of the Parama Shiva.

One who has faith in the true guru's words
steers the mind on to the path of realization.
Such a one rejoices in the
conquest of the senses.
Such a one can never die nor be killed.

Immersed in Shiva, stable of breath,
constant in contemplation.
He whose heart
knows no duality or attachment,
with him alone is the lord of all gurus,
Shiva, delighted.

He is Shiva, Keshava, and Brahma,
eternal and unborn.
May He take away the births and deaths
of this poor woman.
He, Hara, just Hara, the only One!!

III

THE REALIZATION

Like gold when burnished loses all impurities
I glowed bright in the fire of
pure consciousness.
Melting in love,
I found the fog of delusion lift
as the sun rose right beside me!

Steeped in the sounds of Omkara,
I was purified in this furnace.
Giving up the ways of the senses,
I followed the One Path
and reached this place of light.

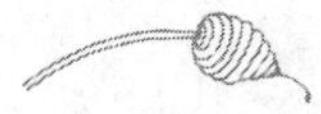

Pure consciousness was such bliss,
all veils of illusion and thought lifted.
Spontaneously I realized my whole Self.
And Lal bloomed like a lotus in the mud.

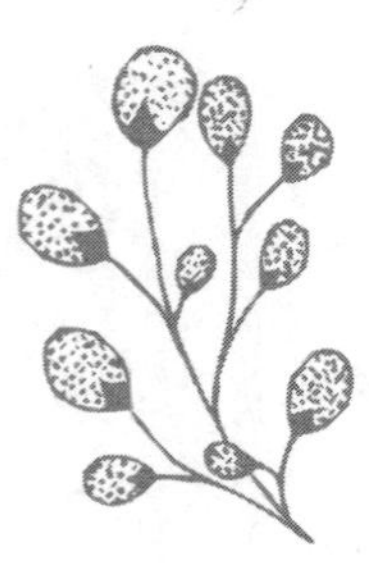

I arrived in this world an ascetic
and spontaneously realized the
light of the Self.
I have severed the cycle of births and deaths.
I now know neither I
nor anyone else really dies.

When it was all about me
I lost sight of you, though
I searched morn to dusk.
Ever since I found you in myself
there's no me, just You, You, only You!

Alert, when Lal entered her heart
she witnessed the union of
Shiva and Shakti there!
She dissolved into an ocean of nectar.
Transcending life while still alive thus, death
had no business with Lal anymore!

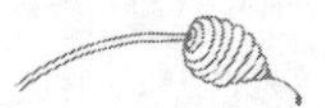

The image of the deity and its pedestal
are both made from the same stone
as is the humble flour-grinder.
Shiva, residing in all, is subtle indeed!

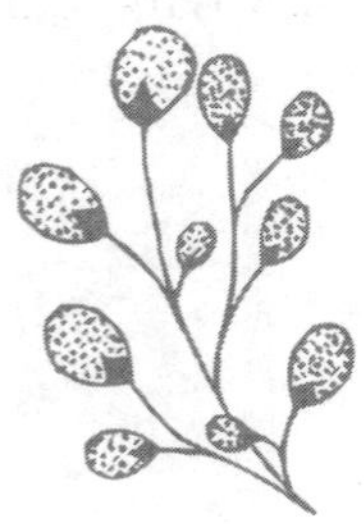

As a mother, He feeds and nourishes us.
As a wife, He pleases and satiates the senses.
As the material world,
He deludes and imprisons us.
Shiva, who is everything, is subtle indeed!

You are gravity,
creating and upholding the earth.
You are the life-force
animating mere skeletons.
You are the pulsating drum-beat of creation
and you the drummer.
God! Who can fathom your measure?

You are the sky, you are the earth.
You are day, night, and the air.
You are the sandalwood,
you the flowers and water.
What can I possibly offer to whom then?

Whose horse is Shiva, Vishnu the saddle
and Brahma the stirrup?
Who is this marvellous horse rider
whom only yogis can recognize
through their powers?

Unstruck reverberation of the universe,
sans name, form, or class.
It is pure I-consciousness
that can ride such a horse!

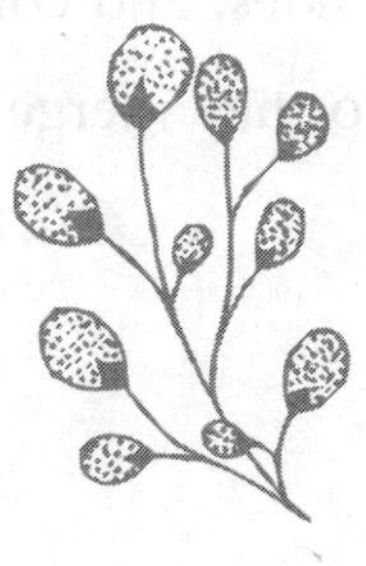

When the sun dissolved, the moon still shone.
When the moon dissolved,
consciousness remained.
When consciousness too disappeared,
nothing remained anywhere.
The earth, the skies, and consciousness—
what do they merge into?

Practices (tantra) gave way to
knowledge (mantra).
Knowledge dissolved into consciousness.
When consciousness dissolved,
nothing remained.
Nothingness dissolved into nothingness!

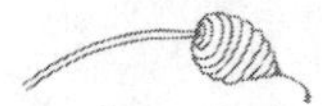

Neither the mind nor speech,
gestures nor silence,
nothing finds entry there.
Shiva and Shakti too aren't to be found there.
That which remains is nothingness!

Neither you nor I, neither meditation
nor its object God.
All actions dissolve away.
Only the One like no other is.
Experiencing the transcendent,
all existence dissolves away!

IV

THE WAY

Believing yourself to be your body
you stayed entangled in its affairs.
You indulged it without end.
But it won't last, not even ashes or its smell.

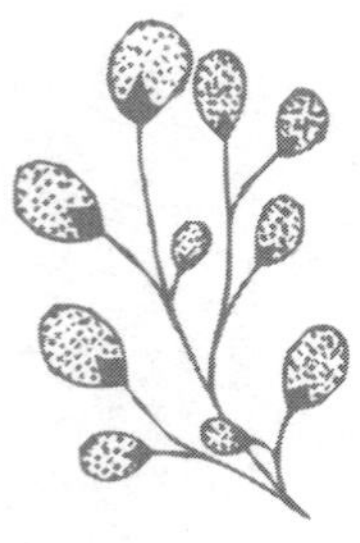

Even while residing in this body,
search for that true essence for which it is
but an abode.
All greed and attachments will be shed then
and your body will glow.

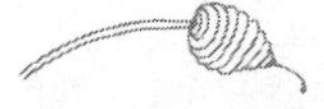

Excessive indulgence will do you no good.
Excessive abstention will breed pride.
Stay the middle course and eat but little.
Moderation will open all doors.

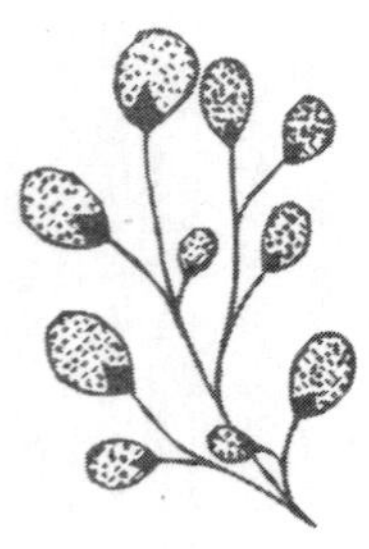

Don't torture the body
with hunger and thirst.
If it weakens, tend to it.
All your efforts and your vows will lie waste
if you do not care for the weak.

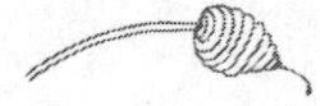

Rituals and fasting are not the real way
nor the adoption of special attire.
Fulfilling bodily desires is not it either.
Contemplate the true Self;
this is the best advice!

Recognize and anticipate lust,
anger and greed,
and destroy them
with good thoughts and self-control.
Or they will destroy you!

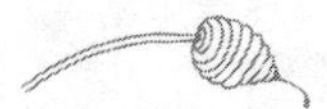

Rid yourself of desires for material objects
and focus on the true Self.
It is not hard to access, and is near you.
Search not far. Just pay attention to It.

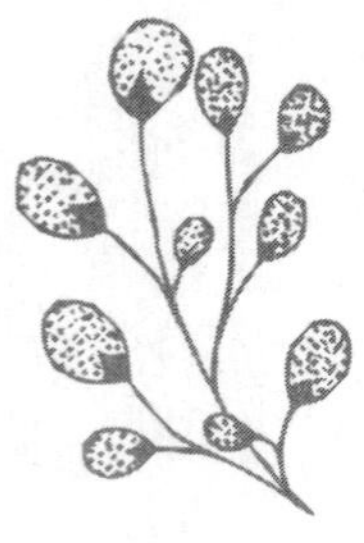

Ego, greed and lust waylay seekers of truth.
The one who triumphs over them
and aspires only to serve
is rid of all worldly attachments.
And seeking spontaneously the ultimate goal,
he or she attains God.

When you were in the womb you knew
a state of pure consciousness.
And were sworn to return to it, do recall!
Cross over in your lifetime,
then, and die to death.

They shield you from the cold
and protect your modesty,
feeding off merely grass and water.
Who on earth offers sentient animals
as sacrifice to insentient deities?

The thoughtless do read the scriptures
and recite them like a parrot in its cage.
What is the purpose
for which they read the Gita?
I read it and am lost in contemplation.

To read scriptures is easy,
to follow them is rare.
The quest for pure consciousness
is not easy but subtle.
Only if practised deeply are scriptures useful.
Then the bliss of pure consciousness
makes its home in the heart.

Just as it is futile to offer jaggery to a donkey
or plant seeds in sand
or butter a cake made of mere husk,
so it is an utter waste to talk spirituality
to an obstinate fool.

The sweet may taste bitter to one
and the bitter sweet to another.
To each his own.
Whoever resolves upon achieving
even a difficult goal
will reach his or her destination for sure!

To fly through the air
or stop the flow of gushing waters,
to douse fire by incantation
or produce milk from a wooden cow—
all such miracles
and show of spiritual prowess
are but chicanery and deceit!

Going on pilgrimage or renouncing the world
as per tradition
will not secure you union with Hari.
Go the pathless way!
Don't fall for illusions.

What is the point of forsaking the home and
heading to the forest?
Why smear sacred ash
and ointments on yourself?
You are fine just the way you are!
Bear God in your heart, that's all it takes!

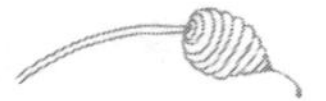

Why thrash about in the dark like one blind?
If you are a Trika, just look within.
That is where Shiva resides, look no further.
Trust me. What I say is spontaneous and true.

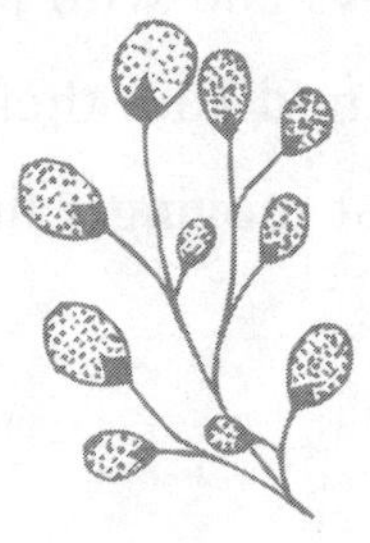

Flowers, kusha-grass, water for oblation,
sesame seeds, a lamp to light—
what are they for when all you need to do,
says my Guru,
is immerse yourself in Shiva,
always and with joy.
You will find Him then easily
without moving a finger.

To oppress or suppress yourself
is not required
to obtain spontaneous liberation.
Nor will merely wishing for it work,
no matter how hard you wish.
You need to experience the spontaneous,
and that is rare!

Chant 'hansah', the spontaneous mantra
which is your breath.
Forget yourself and realize God.
He will appear without a doubt
if you give up your obsession with yourself.

Despite having eyes, be like the blind;
despite learning, like the fool.
Be deaf and mute though
you can hear and speak,
and don't overthink.
Suspending all faculties, just be. Just be!

Deep suffering is calamitous
like a lightning strike
and painful like being crushed in a flour mill.
It is despair like darkness at noon.
But suffer well, for suffering will lighten
the burden that is your ego.

Who worships and who is worshipped?
How does one offer Him to Him?
Which flowers, water or mantra
will awaken Shankara?

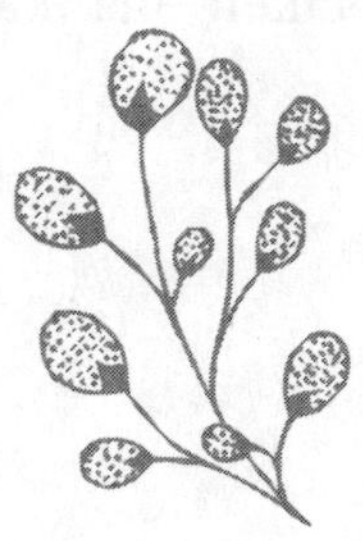

The heart worships,
desire for Him is the driving force.
Offer flowers of emotion,
nectar of pure consciousness
and the mantra of silence
to awaken Shankara.

Uttering Om, focused on the chakra
in the navel,
one can access the universe.
He who has this mantra of consciousness
has no use for any other.

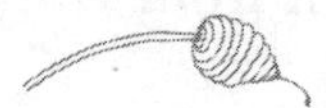

Most subtle is the all-pervading Shiva.
No one knows how He animated
mere skeletons to life.
If you don't realize this when alive,
you hardly will when dead.
Heed what I say:
Free yourself from worldly illusions.

The cold freezes the water
causing snow, sleet and frost.
They are but one, though,
just as for the truly conscious
all of creation is One,
pervaded by Shiva alone.

Whether you yawn, laugh, cough or sneeze
consciousness is always near you.
It bathes in all the holy spots
and reveals itself all the year round
if only you look!

Who dies and for whom?
Who kills and who is killed?
The one who, letting go of Shiva,
chases after life's illusions:
he dies and he is killed.

The mind-stallion races all over the skies.
In a moment it crosses
a hundred thousand leagues.
Seize it! Bind it!
And leash it with your breath,
bringing poise and ease to yourself.

Hunger, thirst or touch no longer bother
the one who masters his life-breath.
Such a one is no longer
subject to worldly births and deaths.

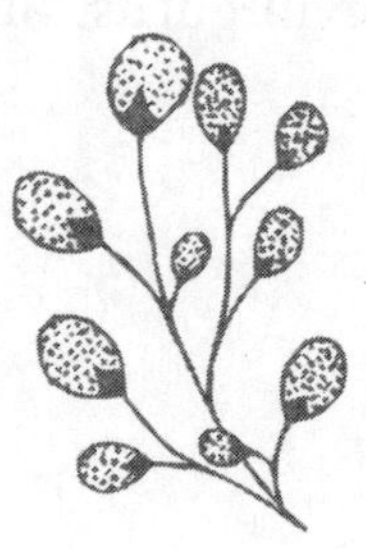

He who sees as one the Self
and the transcendent,
to him day and night are the same,
every direction the same,
and to him alone
does the lord of all gurus, Shiva, manifest.

Shiva is the sole reality and witness in
whichever direction you look.
Never distinguish
the Brahmin and the Muslim then.
If you're a Trika,
go within, know only yourself!

Whether humble or proud,
human nature is like water in a sieve.
True achievement is his who can grasp
the mammoth-like truth of Oneness.

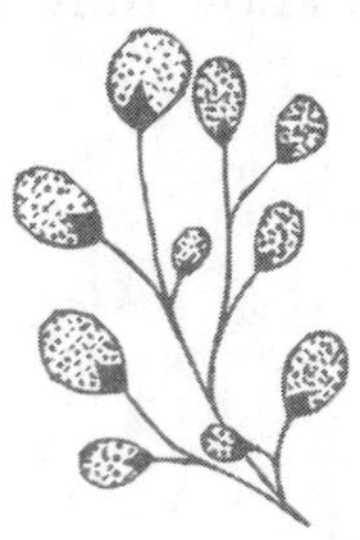

Once you free yourself of the
illusion of worldly time
it doesn't matter whether you are at home
or in a hermitage.
Blemishless God is everywhere you look.
You can realize Him anywhere, anytime!

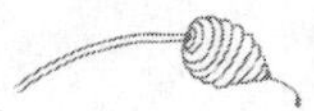

When day ends and night falls,
the earth and the sky become one.
Even the moon
disappears entirely on amavasya.
In the same way, may your consciousness
merge into Shiva!

The noose of worldly life
is tightened by ignorance.
But illumined by the rays of
pure consciousness
you are truly liberated in life.

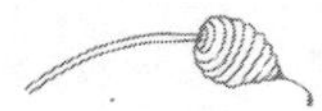

What is ignorance, and what is awareness?
Which lake constantly ebbs and flows?
What is ideal for the worship of Shiva?
What is the highest state and
who may attain it?

The mind is ignorance, Shiva alone awareness.
The five senses are the waters
that forever ebb and flow.
Contemplation of the Self is Shiva worship.
Parama Shiva, the highest state,
is attainable only by pure consciousness.

Some, even when asleep,
are awake to the true reality.
Others, though awake, are as good as asleep.
Some will remain impure,
no matter how often they bathe.
Others will not be affected even as they
perform all worldly duties.

Keep the lamp of your heart aflame
with the nectar of consciousness.
Rid of all doubts, you will then be as content
as an infant in his mother's lap.

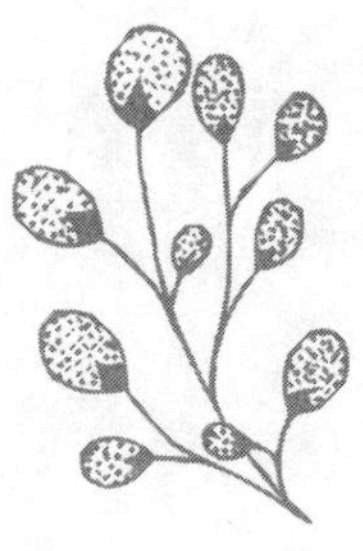

Lal says: all my utterances of wisdom,
judge them for yourself.
Immersion in Omkara will destroy
all causes and all fears of death!

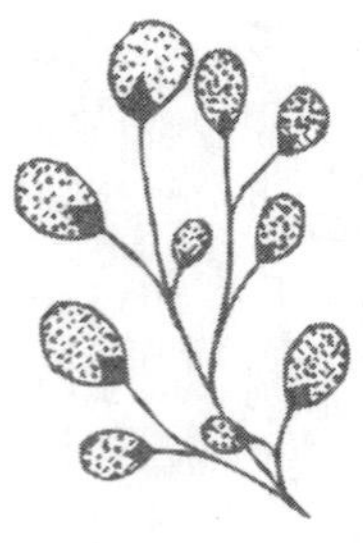